TAKE CHARGE OF YOUR LIFE

BAHAULLA SEKH

Copyright © Bahaulla Sekh
All Rights Reserved.

This book has been self-published with all reasonable efforts taken to make the material error-free by the author. No part of this book shall be used, reproduced in any manner whatsoever without written permission from the author, except in the case of brief quotations embodied in critical articles and reviews.

The Author of this book is solely responsible and liable for its content including but not limited to the views, representations, descriptions, statements, information, opinions and references ["Content"]. The Content of this book shall not constitute or be construed or deemed to reflect the opinion or expression of the Publisher or Editor. Neither the Publisher nor Editor endorse or approve the Content of this book or guarantee the reliability, accuracy or completeness of the Content published herein and do not make any representations or warranties of any kind, express or implied, including but not limited to the implied warranties of merchantability, fitness for a particular purpose. The Publisher and Editor shall not be liable whatsoever for any errors, omissions, whether such errors or omissions result from negligence, accident, or any other cause or claims for loss or damages of any kind, including without limitation, indirect or consequential loss or damage arising out of use, inability to use, or about the reliability, accuracy or sufficiency of the information contained in this book.

Made with ♥ on the Notion Press Platform
www.notionpress.com

Contents

Introduction

"We can let circumstances rule us, or we can take charge and rule our lives from within." — Earl Nightingale

Taking charge of your life is a critical step toward the life you want. It means taking responsibility for the decisions and actions that shape your life and taking thoughtful steps toward the future you want. Here we'll explore what it means to take charge of your life, the benefits of doing so, and the consequences of not taking responsibility for your life. By reading this book, you'll discover practical strategies that will help you take charge of your life and achieve your goals. Let's begin by exploring what it means to take charge of your life.

Taking charge of your life means being in control of your own destiny. It means making conscious choices and taking thoughtful steps toward the life you want. When you take charge of your life, you become responsible for your actions and decisions. You take ownership of your life and actively work to create the future you want. Taking charge of your life is all about being active in making decisions and taking actions that align with your goals and desires. It means taking responsibility for your life instead of letting external factors dictate your path. To take charge of your life, you need to start by setting clear and achievable goals for both the short term and the long term. Once you've determined your goals, create a plan that outlines the actions you need to take to achieve them. Taking action is the next step. Although you have to start with small steps, the most important thing is to take action toward your goals. You must hold yourself accountable for your actions and decisions, and take responsibility for the outcomes. To succeed in taking charge of your life, you also need to be flexible and open to change. Be willing to learn from your mistakes and adjust your plan accordingly. Taking charge of your life is about being in control and taking the necessary actions to shape your destiny. You have the power to create the life you want, so don't be afraid to take the necessary actions to make it happen.

Taking charge of your life can also have a positive effect on your physical health. When you take control of your life, you can adopt healthy behaviors such as regular exercise, a balanced diet, and adequate sleep. These behaviors can improve your overall health and reduce the risk of chronic diseases such as obesity, diabetes, and heart disease. In addition, taking charge of your life can help you reduce unhealthy behaviors such as smoking, excessive alcohol consumption, or drug addiction, which can have negativehealth effects. When you take charge of your life, you become more focused and driven to achieve your goals, which can increase your productivity. You will be more likely to prioritize your time and energy on tasks that align with your values and goals, and less likely to waste time on unproductive or irrelevant activities. Additionally, taking charge of your life can help you develop good time management skills which can increase your effectiveness and efficiency in completing tasks. When you're more productive, you get more done in less time, which can free up time for other activities or hobbies that are important to you.

Taking charge of your life can have a profound and positive impact on all areas of your life, including your sense of purpose, control, well-being, motivation, relationships, physical health, and productivity. By taking responsibility for your actions and choices, and being active in shaping your own destiny, you can create a more fulfilling, rewarding, and meaningful life.

Failing to take charge of your life can lead to missed opportunities and a lack of personal growth. You may find yourself settling for a job or relationship that doesn't satisfy you, or you may find yourself stuck in a cycle of bad habits or behaviors that prevent you from living the life you want. Also if you don't take charge of your life, you can become too dependent on others to make the decision and solve problems, which can lead to feelings of insecurity and a lack of self-confidence. You may also experience a loss of motivation and direction because you may not have a clear idea of what you want out of your life and how to achieve it. In the long run, failing to take charge of your life can have serious consequences on your mental and physical health. It can lead to chronic stress, anxiety, and depression, which can impact your quality of life and even lead to physical illness. Ultimately, taking charge of your life is essential for personal growth, fulfillment, and happiness. It requires courage, self-awareness, self-discipline, and a willingness to make difficult decisions and take risks. By taking charge of your life, you can create a sense of purpose, achieve your goals, and live the life you want.

CHAPTER ONE

VALUES

"It's not hard to make decisions when you know what your values are." — Roy E. Disney

Values are principles and beliefs that guide our thoughts, behaviors, and decisions. These are the things we find important and meaningful in life, and they can have a major impact on how we live and interact with others. The identification of your values is a crucial step in taking charge of your life because they play a key role in shaping your purpose, direction, and fulfillment.

Values are fundamental principles that influence our attitudes and actions. They are the underlying beliefs and ideals that motivate us to pursue certain goals, make certain choices, and prioritize certain areas of our lives over others. Values can be based on many factors such as cultural, religious, social, or personal influences.

Values are important because they act as a compass that guides us to live fulfilling and meaningful life. They give us a sense of direction and purpose, help us make decisions, and inform our relationships with others. When our values align with our actions, we experience authenticity, trust, and satisfaction. Conversely, when our values are not aligned, we may experience inner conflict, dissatisfaction, and restlessness.

Values give meaning and direction to our life. They are guiding principles that influence our attitudes and actions. For example, some people may value honesty, while others may value creativity or kindness. Whatever your values are, they are an integral part of who you are and influence the choices you make in life.

Studies have shown that people living value-based lives generally have higher well-being and more satisfaction in life. A study published in the Journal of Personality and Social Psychology found that people who live according to their values experience greater psychological well-being, including higher self-esteem and less anxiety and depression. The study also found that living a values-driven life is associated with better resilience to stress and adversity.

Kiran Mazumdar-Shaw is an Indian entrepreneur and founder of Biocon, a biopharmaceutical company. She is known for her strong values and ethical leadership, which have helped her build a successful business and have a positive impact on society. Kiran Mazumdar-Shaw's life isn't just about building a successful business, it's about finding strong values and living by them. Throughout her life, Kiran has been guided by a deep commitment to ethics and social responsibility, and this has been key to her success.

Kiran grew up in Bangalore, India, and studied biology at Bangalore University. After graduation, she worked as a brewer at Carlton and United Breweries in Australia, where she gained experience in fermentation technology. In 1978, she returned to India and founded Biocon with a capital of only Rs. 10,000 (about $140 at that time).

One of the most important lessons you can learn from Kiran's story is the importance of finding your values. For Kiran, her values were shaped by her upbringing and experiences as a young scientist and entrepreneur. She saw the potential of biotechnology to positively impact society and was in favor of using that technology to develop affordable and accessible medicines.

This commitment to social responsibility and ethics guided Kiran to build Biocon from a small start-up to a global biopharmaceutical company. Kiran faced many challenges along the way, including a lack of funding, regulatory hurdles, and pressure from investors to maximize profits. However, she never lost sight of her values and refused to compromise on ethics or social responsibility.

For Kiran, finding values and living by them was not only a personal choice but also a smart business strategy. She realized that a values-based approach could help her to create a strong culture of trust and transparency at Biocon, which would ultimately lead to greater success. By prioritizing employee well-being, investing in employee training and development, and staying true to her vision of affordable and accessible healthcare, Kiran has been able to build a sustainable business that truly makes a difference in people's lives.

Biocon is now one of India's largest biopharmaceutical companies with operations in over 120 countries. Kiran's values-driven leadership has helped the company achieve success and made a positive impact on society. Biocon is focused on developing affordable and accessible medicines for those in need, and Kiran is a strong advocate for access and affordability of healthcare in India and around the world.

Kiran's life is a great example of how value-based leadership can lead to success and a positive impact on society. Staying true to her vision and values, Kiran has built a successful business that has a real impact on people's life.

So how do you find values? Like Kiran, our values often change based on our experience, education, and personal beliefs. One way to start is to think about what is most important to us and what we stand for. We can also look to role models like Kiran who embody strong values and seek opportunities to connect with like-minded people and organizations.

By finding our values and living by them, we can not only live a fuller life but also have a positive impact on the world around us. Kiran Mazumdar-Shaw's life is a powerful example of how value-based leadership can lead to success and bring out real change in society.

Understanding your values

To find your values, it is important to think about what is most important to you. For example, if you value honesty, you might ask yourself why honesty is important to you. Maybe it's because you think being honest builds trust, or maybe it's because you think it's the right thing to do. By understanding your values, you can better understand what motivates you and how you can live a more fulfilling life.

Think about what is most important to you, what inspires you, and what makes you feel satisfied.

consider the following questions:

- What are the things that make me happy and fulfilled and why?
- What do I believe in, and why?
- What are my priorities in life and why?
- What motivates me to take action and why?
- What are my strengths and weaknesses, and how do they relate to my values?

Identifying areas where your values conflict with your actions

If you identify areas where your values are not aligned with your choices, it is important to find out why this might be the case. Your decisions may be influenced by external pressures or conflicting values. It can also be helpful to examine the consequences of these choices and determine whether they align with your long-term goals and aspirations.

Once you've determined your values, it's important to assess how they align with your life choices. For example, if you value honesty but find yourself lying to avoid conflict, there may be a conflict between your values and your actions. It is important to recognize these differences and work to align your values with your choices.

consider the following questions:

- Are my current actions and behaviors consistent with my values?
- Am I doing something that the person I see myself would not do?
- Am I living in alignment with what is most important to me?

- Are there any areas of my life where my values are not aligned with my choices?

In conclusion, discovering your values is an important step toward taking charge of your life. Values provide a sense of direction, purpose, and fulfillment, and they play an important role in shaping our attitudes, behaviors, and relationships. By examining your values, evaluating their compatibility with your life choices, and identifying areas where they conflict with your actions, you can experience a more authentic and fulfilled life.

CHAPTER TWO

THE POWER OF A GROWTH MINDSET

"Mindset is what separates the best from rest." — unknown

Do you believe that your abilities and qualities are fixed traits that cannot be developed, or do you believe that they can be improved through hard work and learning? This is the fundamental difference between a fixed mindset and a growth mindset, and it can have a profound impact on your personal and professional growth.

In this chapter, we'll explore why cultivating a growth mindset is essential for overcoming challenges, achieving success, and living a fulfilling life. We'll also explore the negative consequences of a fixed mindset and discuss how to identify and overcome fixed mindset triggers.

David Goggins is a renowned motivational speaker, ultramarathoner, and former Navy SEAL. He has inspired countless people with his remarkable achievements in both physical and mental endurance, becoming an emblem of determination and resilience.

Born in Buffalo, New York, Goggins grew up in a tumultuous household where he suffered abuse from his father. Despite the challenges he faced, he was determined to succeed and enlisted in the US Air Force in 1994. After joining the Tactical Air Control Party, he later became a member of the Navy SEALs, where he served as a communications specialist for SEAL Team Five.

In 2001, Goggins left the military and pursued a career as a professional ultramarathoner, competing in some of the world's most challenging races, including the Badwater Ultramarathon. He set world records for running 101.2 miles in under 20 hours, completing 4,030 pull-ups in 24 hours, and finishing the Ironman World Championship in Hawaii within two months.

Goggins is not only known for his physical prowess but also his inspirational speeches, where he encourages people to push beyond their limits and embrace a growth mindset. He believes in "taking souls" and never giving up, even in the face of adversity. Despite battling obesity, depression, and a severe car accident that left him with a shattered leg, Goggins remains committed to his mission of inspiring others to achieve their goals.

David Goggins' life exemplifies the power of a growth mindset, showing that anything is possible with hard work, dedication, and a never-give-up attitude. He is truly the toughest man alive, and his story is an inspiration to all of us.

The Benefits of a Growth Mindset

People with a growth mindset are more resilient in the face of challenges and failures. They see these obstacles as opportunities for growth and learning, not as signs of their limitations. This way of thinking can increase motivation by focusing on personal success and development rather than external factors such as competition or the approval of others. It also encourages people to think outside the box and explore new ideas and approaches, which increases creativity and innovation. Additionally, a growth mindset can promote healthier relationships by fostering empathy, understanding, and a willingness to learn and grow with others. Research has also shown that a growth mindset is associated with greater success in personal and professional pursuits. People with a growth mindset are more likely to take on new challenges, endure hardship, and achieve their goals. A growing mindset culture can lead to greater personal success, professional advancement, and overall well-being. It helps people see challenges as opportunities for growth and learning and encourages them to approach themselves and others with empathy and understanding.

Difference between a fixed mindset and a growth mindset.

A fixed mindset is a belief system in which people believe that their personal qualities such as intelligence, talent, and abilities are fixed characteristics that cannot be changed or developed. People with a fixed mindset believe that their level of success or failure in any given area is predetermined by their inherent abilities or lack thereof, and they often avoid challenges that could threaten their self-image. In contrast, a growth mindset is a belief system in which people believe that their abilities and qualities can be developed and improved through hard work, practice, and learning. People with a growth mindset see challenges and failures as opportunities to grow and learn and are more likely to take on new challenges and overcome difficulties. The main difference between a fixed mindset and a growth mindset is that people with a fixed mindset believe that their abilities are fixed and cannot be developed, while people with a growth mindset believe that their abilities can be developed and improved through effort and persistence.

Negative consequences of a fixed mindset

A fixed mindset can limit a person's potential for personal and professional growth. People with a fixed mindset may avoid challenges that might reveal their limitations, and may not invest the necessary time and effort to develop new skills or knowledge. This can lead to a fear of failure, negative self-talk, and reduced resilience in the face of adversity or failure. Finally, a fixed mindset can limit a person's success because they may not believe that they have the ability to achieve their goals or they may not be willing to put in the effort to reach their goals.

Identifying Your Fixed Mindset Triggers

Identifying triggers for a fixed mindset can be a useful step in cultivating a growth mindset. Here are some examples of common fixed mindset triggers: When you experience failure or setbacks, you may feel like giving up or believe that you can't succeed.

- **Criticism:** When you receive criticism or negative feedback, you can become defensive and take it personally instead of seeing it as an opportunity to learn and grow.
- **Comparison:** By comparing yourself to others and focusing on their accomplishments, you may feel inadequate and believe you will never achieve.
- **Effort:** If you think success should come easily and quickly, you may give up easily when faced with challenges or setbacks.
- **Limiting beliefs:** If you have deeply held beliefs about your abilities or potential that are negative or self-limiting, these can trigger a fixed mindset.
- **Fear:** Fear of failure, fear of success, or fear of the unknown can all trigger a fixed mindset and prevent you from taking risks and striving for growth.
- **Comfort zone:** If you are content with the status quo and resist change, you are more likely to fall into a fixed mindset and avoid challenges.

By identifying your fixed mindset triggers, you can come to know when you are falling into a fixed mindset and take action to change your mindset to growth. It can help you build resilience, overcome challenges, and achieve your goals.

Overcoming Fixed Mindset Triggers

Overcoming fixed mindset triggers can be a challenging but rewarding process.

The first step to overcoming fixed mindset triggers is to recognize that they are there. Pay attention to the thoughts and feelings that come up when you face challenges or setbacks. Reframe negative thoughts and self-talk. Challenge negative thoughts and replace them with more positive and empowering ones. For example, instead of thinking "I can't do it," try thinking "I can't do it yet, but I will keep trying." Accept challenges as opportunities for growth and learning. Rather than avoiding challenges, seek them out and approach them with a growth mindset. Rather than focusing solely on outcomes, focus on the effort and progress you are making. Celebrate small victories and acknowledge the effort you are putting in.

Instead of rejecting feedback, look for it and use it as an opportunity to learn and grow. Remember that feedback is not a reflection of your value as a person, but rather an opportunity to improve. Be kind to yourself when you experience setbacks or failures. Understand that making mistakes and experiencing failures are a natural part of learning. Try to spend more time with people who have a growth mindset and who will support and encourage you on your journey.

Embracing the Growth Mindset

Believing that intelligence and talent can be developed through hard work, dedication and determination is the essence of the growth mindset. This mindset provides many benefits, including increased resilience, motivation, and success. People who adopt a growth mindset

see setbacks and failures as learning opportunities, which makes them more resilient and better able to overcome obstacles. They also tend to be more driven to seek out challenges and opportunities for growth.

Examples of people with a growth mindset include Elon Musk, the CEO of Tesla and SpaceX, known for his relentless work ethic and spirit of innovation. Despite many challenges, he perseveres towards his goals and always seeks to improve and learn from his experiences. Adopting a growth mindset can have a significant impact on one's life, leading to increased resilience, motivation, and success. By focusing on effort and growth rather than innate abilities, people can overcome challenges and reach their full potential.

Developing a Growth Mindset

Developing a growth mindset may require effort and time, but there are actionable steps that can help you achieve it. Rather than avoiding challenges, seek them out as opportunities to learn and grow. Challenge yourself to learn new things and step outside of your comfort zone.

Instead of focusing solely on results, concentrate on the effort you put into your work. Recognize that growth and development require hard work and dedication. Rather than seeing failures as a reflection of personal shortcomings, see them as opportunities for growth. Take the time to analyze what went wrong and identify ways to improve for next time.

Use the power of "yet" to cultivate a growth mindset. When faced with a new skill or challenge, acknowledge that you haven't yet mastered it, but can improve with effort and practice. Embrace a learning mindset by viewing every experience as an opportunity to learn something new. Seek feedback, ask questions, and be open to new perspectives and ideas.

If you're looking to develop a growth mindset, there are several practices you can adopt. One effective strategy is journaling, which involves reflecting on your experiences and challenges and identifying areas for improvement. Writing down your goals and the steps you need to take to achieve them can also help you stay focused and motivated.

Another helpful practice is gratitude, which involves focusing on the positive aspects of your life and recognizing the progress you've made toward your goals. Visualizing yourself achieving your goals and the steps needed to get there can also help you build confidence and motivation. Mindfulness meditation is another tool that can help you manage stress and anxiety, cultivate a sense of inner calm and focus, and stay present at the moment. Additionally, challenging yourself to learn new skills or take on new hobbies can help you embrace the process of learning and improving over time.

However, several obstacles can hinder the cultivation of a growth mindset. These include fear of failure, lack of support, fixed mindset beliefs, negative self-talk, and lack of motivation. To overcome these obstacles, it's important to reframe failure as an opportunity for growth and learning, seek out positive influences, challenge fixed mindset beliefs, practice positive affirmations, break your goals down into smaller steps, and celebrate your successes along the way.

CHAPTER THREE

SETTING GOALS

"Setting goals is the first steps in turning the invisible into the visible." — Tony Robbins

Setting goals is one of the most important steps to achieving success in all areas of life. Goals provide direction, focus, and motivation to help people stay on track and achieve desired results. In this chapter, we'll explore the importance of goal setting, the different types of goals, Setting SMART goals, and creating a plan to achieve your goals.

Tony Robbins is an outstanding example of a person who sets and accomplishes goals. Robbins is a renowned motivational speaker, life coach, and author who has assisted millions of people in achieving their personal and professional objectives.

Robbins is a strong believer in the importance of goal setting, and he has created a system for establishing and accomplishing goals that have been widely embraced around the world. He believes that setting specific, measurable, and achievable objectives is essential for success in all aspects of life.

Throughout his career, Robbins has established and accomplished numerous objectives, including establishing a successful coaching company, writing best-selling books, and becoming a sought-after public speaker. He has also utilized his platform to assist others in setting and achieving their objectives through his coaching programs, books, and seminars.

Robbins' work with Canadian Olympic gold medalist Donovan Bailey is an excellent example of his goal-setting success. Bailey was struggling with injuries and had lost his confidence as a sprinter in 1996. Robbins helped Bailey set a specific objective - to win the gold medal in the 100-meter dash at the 1996 Summer Olympics in Atlanta - using his goal-setting system.

Robbins assisted Bailey in visualizing himself winning the race, creating a plan for achieving his objective, and staying focused and motivated throughout the training process. The result was one of the most unforgettable moments in Olympic history, as Bailey won the gold medal in a record-breaking time of 9.84 seconds.

Tony Robbins has become a strong proponent of the power of goal-setting through his success and his work with others. His story demonstrates that by setting specific, measurable, and achievable objectives and taking consistent action towards those objectives, we can achieve success in any area of our life.

The Importance of Setting Goals

Setting goals provides clarity by defining what you want to accomplish. When you have a clear understanding of your objectives, you can create a roadmap toward success. Goals also motivate action by inspiring you to take steps towards achieving your desired outcomes, pushing you out of your comfort zone and into new opportunities. Goals also enhance productivity by helping you prioritize your time and resources. By focusing on what's important, you can maximize your efficiency and achieve more in less time. Goals enhance decision-making by providing a framework for making choices that align with your objectives. This allows you to make informed decisions that support your goals and move you closer to achieving them. Setting goals also promotes accountability by tracking your progress toward your goals, which makes you more likely to stay committed and take responsibility for your actions. This accountability helps you stay motivated and on track toward achieving your desired outcomes. Lastly, goals foster personal growth by challenging you to step outside of your comfort zone and learn new skills. When you set ambitious goals, you can push yourself to grow and develop in new and exciting ways.

Setting goals is an essential component of taking charge of your life. The meta-analytic review published in 2019 investigated the efficiency of goal setting in a variety of contexts, including schooling, sports, and work. The evaluation included 144 research and discovered that setting specific and difficult goals was connected with higher levels of performance across different situations. The analysis also discovered that adding feedback, goal commitment, and complexity to goals improved goal setting's effectiveness. The study adds to the body of evidence that SMART goal setting can be an effective technique for obtaining targeted objectives.

By defining your objectives, staying focused, and taking action, you can achieve success and personal growth in all areas of your life. So, take charge of your life by setting goals that align with your passions and purpose, and watch as you move closer to your dreams and aspirations.

Types of Goals and Why

When it comes to goals setting, it's important to choose the right kind of goals that aligns with your personal preferences and values. By setting goals that align with your values and aspirations, you can find direction and meaning in your life. You can set a variety of goals for yourself, including short-term goals, long-term goals, personal development goals, career goals, financial goals, relationship goals, and health and wellness goals.

Knowing why you want to accomplish what you want to accomplish is critical because it provides a feeling of purpose and motivation. You are more likely to remain dedicated in the face of difficulties and disappointments if you have a clear knowledge of your why. Knowing why you want to accomplish your goals can enable you to make decisions that are in line with your values and aspirations.

Also, knowing why you do what you do might help you make more meaningful and practical goals. When you understand the motivations behind your goals, you can modify your plan to suit your unique requirements. It will be more enjoyable and rewarding to work towards something that is consistent with your passion and principles. In addition, Knowing why you do what you do might help you push through challenges and overcome setbacks. Remembering why you initially set out to accomplish that objective will help you maintain your motivation when faced with obstacles.

Understanding why you want to achieve what you want to do is crucial for remaining motivated, making wise decisions, setting meaningful goals, and overcoming obstacles. You can work towards a more fulfilling existence by becoming aware of your own motives, which will allow you to match your actions with your goals.

SMART Goal Setting

Setting goals is an important step towards taking charge of your life, but setting SMART goals is even more effective. SMART is an acronym that stands for Specific, Measurable, Achievable, Relevant, and Time-bound. Let's break down each of these components and see how they work:

- **Specific:** Your goal should be specific and clearly defined. For example, instead of setting a goal to "exercise more," a specific goal would be "to jog for 30 minutes, three times a week."
- **Measurable:** Your goal should be measurable so that you can track your progress. In the example above, the progress can be measured by tracking the number of times you jogged for 30 minutes each week.
- **Achievable:** Your goal should be realistic and achievable. For example, if you've never jogged before, setting a goal to run a marathon in a month is not achievable. Instead, start with a goal that is challenging but achievable, like the one above.
- **Relevant:** Your goal should be relevant to your aspirations and values. In the example above, if your value is to live a healthy and active lifestyle, jogging three times a week is relevant to that value.
- **Time-bound:** Your goal should have a deadline or timeframe for completion. In the example above, the goal has a timeframe of one week, but you could set

a larger time frame, such as two or three months, depending on the goal.

By using the SMART framework to set goals, you can achieve your dreams and aspirations more effectively. Remember to create a plan of action and take consistent steps toward achieving your goals. With SMART goals and a clear plan of action, you can take charge of your life and achieve your biggest dreams and aspirations.

Create a Plan

Developing a clear plan of action is crucial for achieving your goals. Without a plan, your goals may remain elusive. To create a solid plan, you should begin by defining your goal in a clear and specific manner. This will help you focus your efforts and keep your eye on the prize. You should then break your goal down into smaller, achievable steps to avoid feeling overwhelmed. It's also important to identify the resources you need, such as time, money, skills, or support from others. Setting a timeline with deadlines for each step will help you stay accountable and focused. Tracking your progress regularly and celebrating your successes will also help you stay motivated. Finally, remind yourself of the benefits of achieving your goal of staying motivated and overcoming obstacles.

For example, let's say you want to learn a new language. Here are some steps you could take to develop a plan of action:

- **Define your goal:** "Learn conversational Spanish."
- **Divide your goal into smaller steps:** Download a language-learning app, practice 20 minutes a day, read

books in Spanish, watch Spanish movies, etc.

- **Identify the resources you need:** A language-learning app, books in Spanish, access to Spanish movies, etc.
- **Set a timeline:** Use the language-learning app daily for three months, read one book in Spanish every two months, and watch one Spanish movie per month.
- **Track your progress:** Regularly assess your progress towards your goal, such as completing app modules or finishing a book.
- **Stay motivated:** Stay motivated by thinking about the benefits of learning a new language, such as being able to travel confidently and connect with new people.

CHAPTER FOUR

HABITS

"We are what we repeatedly do. Excellence, then, is not an act, but a habit." — Aristotle

Success is not a one-time event rather it is the consequence of persistent efforts and wholesome routines formed over time. A habit is any repetitive behavior that is a part of your daily routine. Our daily routines are very important and may either make or destroy us. Cultivating healthy habits can help us achieve success in many aspects of our lives, from our careers to our relationships. In this chapter, we will explore the importance of habits in achieving success, how to break bad habits, and how to develop new, positive habits.

Michael Jordan, widely regarded as one of the greatest basketball players of all time, was known for his unwavering focus and commitment to his craft. He had a strong habit of dedicating himself to practice, spending hours upon hours working on every aspect of his game. Even after his teammates had left, he remained in the gym, perfecting his shooting, dribbling, footwork, and conditioning. In fact, he made it a point to shoot 100 free throws every day before leaving the gym.

Jordan's unwavering dedication to practice paid off tremendously, with winning an impressive six NBA championships, five MVP awards, and making the All-Star team a record 14 times during his career. His rigorous work ethic and ability to perform exceptionally well when it mattered the most left an unforgettable impression on all who witnessed him play.

Not only was Jordan's commitment to basketball unrivaled, but he also maintained strict habits regarding his fitness and health. He followed a strict diet, avoiding unhealthy foods and alcohol to stay in peak physical condition. Additionally, he had a challenging workout routine that he did every day, including on game days.

Jordan's habits and dedication to his craft have inspired numerous fans and athletes around the world. He has become a legendary figure in the world of basketball, and his legacy continues to thrive.

The Importance of Habits in Achieving Success

We can stay focused and organized thanks to our habits. We may stay focused on what needs to be done by creating constructive habits such as time management, task prioritization, and goal setting. We are less likely to get distracted and can focus on the task at hand if we have a clear plan in place.

To succeed, you must be consistent in your efforts. Even when we lack motivation, habits enable us to establish routines and maintain them. Healthy habits emerge naturally from our regular activities. Even in the face of obstacles, this consistency allows us to make progress toward our goals.

Positive habits create momentum, and momentum creates progress. By consistently engaging in productive habits, we build momentum toward achieving our goals. This momentum helps us overcome obstacles and push through difficult times, ultimately leading to success.

Habits also create a positive mindset. Reinforcing positive behavior through habits helps us develop a more confident, motivated, and capable mindset, enabling us to stay focused and persevere through challenges.

Developing positive habits is essential for achieving success. They help us stay organized and focused, create consistency, build momentum, and develop a positive mindset. By consistently engaging in positive habits, we can make progress toward our goals and achieve success over time.

Break Bad Habits

Breaking negative habits might be difficult but it is crucial for personal development. Identifying a problematic habit is the first step toward kicking it. For example, When you are anxious, you may notice that you spend too much time reading through social media or chewing your nails. Recognize the bad habits triggers, such as certain feelings or circumstances, which cause the action. For example, you may discover that boredom triggers your social media scrolling or that worry triggers your nail-biting. If you are aware of the triggers, you may either avoid them or come up with other solutions. Creating a substitute habit that can take the place of the undesirable habit is crucial. When you're bored, you might, for example, replace social media browsing with reading a book or going for a stroll. Instead of chewing your nails, try deep breathing or squeezing a stress ball. Have a plan for how you're going to quit the bad habit and start the new one. For instance, you may arrange time each day for your replacement habit and set a time limit on your social media use. Also, try to tell someone you trust about your strategy, and ask them to hold you accountable. You may, for instance, ask a buddy to watch you every day and encourage you. It takes time and effort to break a bad habit. Be kind to yourself and persevere even if you make mistakes. Think about why it happened and change your strategy, for instance, if you unintentionally spend more time on social media than you anticipated.

Breaking a bad habit and replacing it with a positive one requires self-awareness, determination, and a plan of action. By identifying the habit, understanding the triggers, setting a replacement habit, making a plan, staying accountable, and being patient and persistent, you can successfully break a bad habit and replace it with a positive one.

Develop New Positive Habits

Developing new positive habits can be difficult, but with the right approach and persistence, it's possible. The first step in developing positive habits is to identify the habits you want to develop. For example, let's say you want to get into the habit of reading for at least 30 minutes every day. Once you've identified your habit, it's important to break it down into achievable goals. For example, start with reading for 10 minutes a day and gradually increase the time as you progress. Developing a new habit requires a plan. Make a plan that outlines how you will form the habit, when you will do it, and what you must do to achieve it. In this example, you can schedule a book to read 10 minutes before bed each day. Start with small changes in your routine. This will help you get used to new habits without feeling overwhelmed. For this example, start with reading for 10 minutes a day and gradually increase the time to 30 minutes. Consistency is key to developing a positive habit. Try to stick to your plan, and if you slip up, don't give up. Get back on track as soon as possible. In our example, if you miss a day of reading, get back to it the next day and continue with the habit. Tracking your progress can help you see how far you've come and motivate you to keep going. In this example, you can track the number of days read for at least 10 minutes and gradually increase the time. Rewarding yourself when you reach your goals will help you stay motivated and make the habit more enjoyable. In our example, you can reward yourself with a favorite snack or a relaxing activity after reading for 30 minutes every day for a week. Surrounding yourself with people who support your new habit and creating a positive environment will help you stay on track. In our example, you can join a book club or find a reading buddy who shares your interests.

Developing positive habits takes time and effort. Use the example of developing a habit of reading every day to apply these steps to your own life and start developing positive habits that align with your goals.

Developing healthy habits is essential for personal growth and success. By breaking bad habits and developing new, positive habits, you can take charge of your life and achieve your full potential. Remember that habits take time to develop, so be patient and persistent. With the right mindset and actions, you can create the life you want and deserve.

CHAPTER FIVE

TIME MANAGEMENT

"You will never find time for anything. If you want time, you must make it."— Charles Buxton

One of the most valuable things we have is time, and learning to manage it effectively is essential for taking charge of your life. By mastering time management skills, you can increase your productivity, reduce stress, and achieve greater success and happiness. In this chapter, we will explore the importance of time management and provide you with strategies to manage your time effectively.

A person renowned for his remarkable time management skills is the former President of the United States, Barack Obama. As the leader of a powerful nation, he had an incredibly hectic schedule, yet he managed to balance his professional and personal life with great precision.

One of the key strategies employed by Obama in managing his time was his ability to prioritize tasks. He would identify the most crucial responsibilities and ensure that they were completed before moving on to less pressing matters. Moreover, he was known for utilizing his spare time effectively, such as reading briefing materials while traveling on Air Force One or engaging in early-morning workouts to stay focused and energized. Another critical aspect of Obama's time management was his adeptness at delegating tasks. He recognized the limitations of what he could accomplish alone and delegated certain responsibilities to his team, freeing up his time to focus on high-level decisions and important meetings.

Despite the extraordinary demands of his job, Obama made it a priority to spend quality time with his family. He ensured he was present for dinner with his family as often as possible, and he took breaks from his work schedule to attend his daughters' sporting events and other activities.

Overall, Obama's time management skills allowed him to be highly effective in his role as President while still making time for his family and personal life. His example serves as an inspiration to many striving to achieve success while maintaining a healthy work-life balance.

The ability to manage your time effectively will enable you to accomplish your goals and live a more balanced life. You can learn to prioritize your responsibilities, avoid distractions, and remain on track by working with a coach or practicing time management skills on your own.

The importance of time management

Effective time management is essential to achieving success in both personal and professional life. Time management can help people concentrate on crucial tasks and accomplish them more quickly, resulting in increased levels of productivity. Stress and anxiety can be caused by poor time management. People can experience less stress and a greater sense of control over their lives by efficiently managing their time. People must prioritize tasks and choose how to spend their time in order to manage their time effectively, which improves their decision-making abilities.

Time management enables people to reconcile their personal and professional duties, resulting in a healthy work-life balance. Getting things done and meeting deadlines can increase confidence and self-esteem. Those who are good at managing their time attain their goals and have greater self-confidence.

Identifying time-wasting activities

Efficient time management requires the identification of unproductive tasks that impede productivity. Those tasks don't contribute to objectives and should be reduced or removed. Examples of such tasks include spending excessive time on social media, procrastinating, indulging in gossip, and binge-watching shows.

Eliminating such tasks can create more time to concentrate on productive tasks, which increases productivity, reduces stress, and enhances self-worth. Monitoring daily activities and assessing their contribution to objectives can aid in recognizing these unproductive tasks.

Removing time-wasting tasks is a vital aspect of effective time management. This will allow more time to be allocated to productive tasks, resulting in higher productivity and greater achievement of goals.

Strategies for prioritizing your time

The Eisenhower Matrix is a powerful time management tool that can help you prioritize your tasks based on their level of importance and urgency. This matrix was developed by former U.S. President Dwight D. Eisenhower, who used it to make critical decisions during his presidency.

The Eisenhower Matrix is a four-quadrant grid that categorizes tasks based on their level of importance and urgency. The quadrants are labeled as follows:

	Important	**Not important**
Urgent	*Do First* • Meeting an important deadline • Responding to an urgent email or phone call • Handling a critical customer issue	*Delegate* • Delegating a project to a team member • Outsourcing administrative tasks to a virtual assistant • Assigning a task to a colleague with more expertise in that area
Not Urgent	*Schedule* • Planning and scheduling future projects • Updating a long-term strategic plan • Scheduling time for personal development or self-care activities	*Don't Do* • Spending excessive time on social media or other distractions • Attending meetings that don't add value • Engaging in gossip or other unproductive activities

- **Do First:** Tasks in this quadrant are both urgent and important and require immediate attention. These tasks should be your top priority.
- **Delegate:** This quadrant includes tasks that are not important but urgent. These tasks can be delegated to others, freeing up time for more urgent matters.
- **Schedule:** This quadrant includes tasks that are not urgent but still important. These tasks can be scheduled to be completed at a later time.
- **Don't Do:** This quadrant includes tasks that are neither important nor urgent. These tasks can be eliminated or postponed indefinitely.

By using the Eisenhower Matrix, you can prioritize your tasks more effectively and use your time and energy on the most important and urgent tasks. To use the Eisenhower Matrix, start by listing all the tasks you need to complete. Next, place each task into the appropriate quadrant based on its level of importance and urgency. Finally, prioritize your tasks by focusing on those in the Urgent and Important quadrant first and then moving on to the other quadrants as necessary.

Techniques for managing time

Here we'll discuss the Pomodoro Technique, a time management method that involves breaking down work into intervals of 25 minutes with short breaks in between. The Pomodoro Technique is a time management method that helps you stay focused and productive by breaking down your work into intervals of 25 minutes, called "pomodoros," with short breaks in between. This technique was developed by Francesco Cirillo in the late 1980s and is now widely used by individuals and organizations around the world.

To use the Pomodoro Technique, follow these steps:

- Choose a task to work on.
- Set a timer for 25 minutes and start working on the task.
- When the timer goes off, take a short break of 3-5 minutes.
- Repeat the process, working for 25 minutes and taking short breaks until you have completed four pomodoros.
- After completing four pomodoros, take a longer break of 15-30 minutes.

The idea behind the Pomodoro Technique is to help you stay focused and avoid distractions by breaking your work into manageable intervals. The short breaks allow you to rest and recharge, while the longer breaks give you time to reflect on your progress and plan for the next session. The Pomodoro Technique can be used for any type of work, from studying and writing to coding and designing. It is especially helpful for tasks that require sustained focus and concentration, as well as tasks that can easily become overwhelming or monotonous. By using the Pomodoro Technique, you can increase your productivity, improve your focus, and reduce stress and burnout. It can also help you manage your time more effectively by allowing you to break down your work into smaller, more manageable chunks.

Create a Schedule

Creating a schedule that works for you is an important part of time management. A good schedule should be realistic, flexible, and aligned with your goals.

Here are some tips for creating a good schedule:

- **Identify your goals and priorities:** Before creating a schedule, it's important to identify your goals and priorities. This will help you determine which tasks are most important and should be given priority in your schedule.
- **Use a planner or scheduling tool:** There are many tools available for scheduling, such as physical planners, online calendars, and scheduling apps. Choose a tool that works best for you and use it consistently to keep track of your schedule.
- **Block out time for important tasks:** When creating your schedule, block out time for important tasks first. This will ensure that you prioritize the tasks that are most important to you and give them the attention they deserve.
- Build in flexibility: It's important to build in flexibility to your schedule to accommodate unexpected events or changes in your plans. Leave some open time slots in your schedule to allow for flexibility and adjust your schedule as needed.

• Be realistic: When creating your schedule, be realistic about the amount of time you have available for each task. Don't try to cram too much into your schedule, as this can lead to stress and burnout. Instead, be realistic about what you can accomplish in a given amount of time.

• Review and adjust regularly: Finally, it's important to review and adjust your schedule regularly to ensure that it's working for you. Evaluate how well you're sticking to your schedule and adjust it as needed to better align with your goals and priorities.

CHAPTER SIX

EMOTIONAL INTELLIGENCE

"Emotional intelligence is your ability to recognize and understand emotions in yourself and others, and your ability to use this awareness to manage your behavior and relationships." — Travis Bradberry

Emotional intelligence is the ability to recognize, understand and manage our own emotions, as well as those of others. It involves being aware of our emotional states and how they affect our thoughts and behavior and also being able to empathize with and respond to the emotions of others. Emotional intelligence is an important skill that can help us navigate social relationships, work effectively with others, and lead a fulfilling life.

There is one person who is widely revered for his outstanding emotional intelligence - the Dalai Lama. As the spiritual leader of the Tibetan people, he is known for his remarkable empathy, compassion, and ability to regulate his own emotions, even in challenging situations.

Throughout his life, the Dalai Lama has shown exceptional emotional intelligence, utilizing his skills to create bridges between cultures, religions, and political groups. He has engaged with world leaders, including several US presidents, to advocate for peace and human rights, and has worked tirelessly to foster dialogue and mutual understanding among different communities.

One of the most impressive displays of his emotional intelligence is his response to the Chinese occupation of Tibet. Despite being forced to flee his homeland and live in exile, the Dalai Lama has consistently advocated for non-violent solutions to the conflict, emphasizing the importance of forgiveness, compassion, and understanding.

Another notable example of his emotional intelligence is his collaboration with the Mind and Life Institute, which brings together scientists and contemplative practitioners to explore the relationship between the mind, consciousness, and emotions. Through this partnership, the Dalai Lama has helped to promote a deeper understanding of the nature of emotions, well-being, and the brain, and has inspired countless people to cultivate their emotional intelligence and compassion.

The Dalai Lama's life and teachings continue to inspire people around the world to develop their skills in this area.

Let's examine how we can use emotional intelligence in the world of business. A leader with high emotional intelligence is often more effective in managing their team and achieving their goals. For instance, a socially conscious manager may take the time to

learn each team member's requirements and motivations and tailor their leadership style to their personality. Similarly, a leader who is strong at self-regulation may remain calm and focused under pressure, avoiding impulsive actions that could have bad effects. Another example of emotional intelligence is in personal relationships. A person who is skilled in self-awareness might take the time to understand their emotional triggers and work to manage them to prevent arguments or misunderstandings with their partner. Similarly, someone with relationship management skills might use their emotional intelligence to handle problems in a healthy and constructive way rather than allowing their emotions to rule them.

Emotional intelligence is an important skill for success in both personal and professional life. People with high emotional intelligence are often more effective leaders, better communicators, and better able to work effectively in teams. Emotional intelligence can also improve our physical and mental health, by helping us to manage stress and improve our relationships with others.

There are four key components of emotional intelligence: self-awareness, self-regulation, social awareness, and relationship management.

Self-awareness

Self-awareness involves being able to recognize and understand our own emotions, as well as our strengths and limitations. It includes being aware of our values, motivations, and goals. Self-awareness allows us to better understand ourselves and make more informed decisions about how we want to live our lives. Throughout the day, try to be mindful of your thoughts and feelings. Take note of any changes in your mood or emotional state. At the end of each day, take a few minutes to reflect on your feelings. Think about what situations or events caused you to experience strong emotions, and how you reacted to them. Pay attention to your behavior and actions. Ask yourself why you acted a certain way in a particular situation. Were your actions consistent with your values and goals? Ask trusted friends or family members for feedback on your behavior and how you present yourself to others. This can help you identify blind spots or areas where you may need to improve. Mindfulness meditation can help you become more aware of your thoughts and feelings. By observing your thoughts and feelings without judgment, you can better understand your patterns of behavior. Remember, practicing self-awareness is an ongoing process. By becoming more aware of your thoughts, feelings, and behavior, you can identify areas for improvement and continue to develop your emotional intelligence.

Self-regulation

Self-regulation involves being able to control our emotions and behavior in response to different situations. This includes managing our impulses, the ability to delay gratification, and staying calm and focused under pressure. Self-regulation allows us to make rational decisions and avoid making decisions based solely on our emotions. Identifying our emotional triggers is an important step in developing emotional intelligence. Once you know what triggers your emotions, you can work on managing them. When you feel strong emotions, take a moment to pause before responding. It can help you to avoid reacting impulsively and saying or doing something you may regret. Deep breathing is a simple but effective way to calm your body and regulate your emotions. Take a few deep breaths before responding to a stressful situation. When you experience negative thoughts or emotions, try to reframe them in a more positive light. It can help you see the situation from a different perspective and avoid getting stuck in a negative cycle. Activities such as yoga, meditation, or spending time in nature can help you relax and manage stress. Find an activity that works for you and incorporate it into your routine. Setting clear boundaries can help you manage stress and regulate your emotions. Learn to say no when you need to, and prioritize self-care activities such as exercise, sleep, and time with loved ones. Remember that practicing self-regulation takes time and effort. But by developing these habits, you can better manage your emotions and improve your relationships with others.

Social awareness

Social awareness involves being able to understand the emotions and perspectives of others. This includes being able to read nonverbal cues, such as facial expressions and body language, and being able to listen actively with empathy. Social awareness allows us to better understand and connect with others, which can improve our relationships and our ability to work effectively with others. Pay attention to how other people behave and interact with each other. Observe body language, tone of voice, and facial expressions to better understand their emotions. Put yourself in other people's shoes and try to see things from their point of view. This can help you better understand their emotions and respond with more compassion. When you are interacting with others, make an effort to actively listen. Ask open-ended questions and think about what the person is saying to show you understand.

Nonverbal cues such as body language, tone of voice, and facial expressions can provide important clues about how someone is feeling. Learn to read these cues to better understand the emotions of others. Different cultures have different norms and values. Make an effort to learn about other cultures and be respectful of their customs and

traditions. Your behavior can have a significant impact on others. Be aware of how you present yourself and how your behavior may be perceived by others.

Remember that developing social awareness takes time and effort. But by becoming more attuned to the emotions of others, you can improve your relationships and become a more effective communicator.

Relationship management

Relationship management involves being able to use our emotional intelligence to build and maintain positive relationships with others. This includes the ability to communicate effectively, resolve conflicts, and build trust and rapport. Relationship management allows us to build strong, supportive relationships that can help us achieve our goals and lead fulfilling lives. Effective communication is key to building strong relationships. Be clear, concise, and respectful in your communication with others. Trust is the foundation of any healthy relationship. Be reliable and consistent in your interactions with others, and keep your commitments. Collaboration is working with others to achieve a common goal. Be open to the ideas and perspectives of others and work together to find solutions. Conflicts are inevitable in any relationship. Learn how to handle conflicts healthily by listening actively, being respectful, and working together to find a solution. Holding grudges can hurt relationships. Learn to forgive others for their mistakes, and be willing to apologize when you make mistakes yourself. Don't wait for problems to arise to act. Be proactive in maintaining and strengthening your relationships by checking in regularly and addressing any issues as they arise.

Remember, building and maintaining healthy relationships takes effort and practice. By developing your relationship management skills, you can become a more effective communicator and build stronger, more meaningful connections with others.

By developing your emotional intelligence, you can take charge of your life and achieve greater success and happiness. Emotional intelligence can help you become a more effective communicator, make better decisions, and manage stress more effectively. It can also help you become a better leader and succeed in your career.

CHAPTER SEVEN

Positive Relationships

"You're the average of the five people spend the most time with," — Jim Rohn

As human beings, we are social creatures and relationships have a significant impact on our lives, both in positive and negative ways. Positive relationships can enhance our well-being, reduce stress, and give us a sense of belonging and connection. On the other hand, negative relationships can lead to emotional distress, anxiety, and even physical health issues. It's important to recognize the impact that relationships can have on our lives so that we can make informed choices about the people we choose to spend time with and how we interact with them. Therefore, it's important to cultivate positive relationships in our lives, whether with family members, friends, romantic partners, or colleagues.

Let me tell you about Ruth Bader Ginsburg. She was an Associate Justice of the Supreme Court of the United States from 1993 until she died in 2020.

Throughout her career, Justice Ginsburg was known for her intelligence, perseverance, and dedication to justice. She was one of only nine women in her class at Harvard Law School, and she went on to become the first tenured female professor at Columbia Law School.

In 1980, she was appointed to the United States Court of Appeals for the District of Columbia Circuit, where she served until her appointment to the Supreme Court. During her time on the bench, Justice Ginsburg was a tireless advocate for women's rights, voting rights, and equal protection under the law.

One of the things that made Justice Ginsburg so remarkable was her ability to build bridges across political and ideological divides. Despite her reputation as a liberal icon, she was known for her warm and respectful relationships with her conservative colleagues on the Supreme Court. She famously shared a close friendship with the late Justice Antonin Scalia, despite their vastly different judicial philosophies.

In addition to her legal work, Justice Ginsburg was also known for her personal relationships. She was married to her husband, Martin, for 56 years until his death in 2010. They had two children together, and she often spoke publicly about the support and love that he provided her throughout her career.

Justice Ruth Bader Ginsburg was a remarkable person who made an enormous impact on the world through her dedication to justice and her ability to build meaningful relationships across political and ideological divides.

Building positive relationships is critical to success in many areas of life, including in professional settings. By showing genuine interest and appreciation for others, and making a point to follow up and strengthen relationships over time, people can build strong, positive relationships that can help them achieve their goals.

Identifying Toxic Relationships

Toxic relationships can be harmful to our mental and physical health. Identifying toxic relationships is the first step in removing them from our lives.

Some signs of a toxic relationship are:

- Constantly feeling drained or exhausted after spending time with a person
- Feeling like you're walking on eggshells around the person, afraid to say or do anything that might upset them
- Feeling manipulated, controlled, or pressured by the person
- Feeling that the person does not respect your boundaries or needs
- Feelings like you're always giving, but never receiving anything in return
- Feel like the person does not supportive of your goals or well-being

Trust

Trust is the foundation of any positive relationship. When we trust someone, we feel comfortable and safe around them, and we're more likely to share our thoughts and emotions with them. It takes time and effort to build trust, but we can do this by being honest and transparent in our communication, keeping our promises, and respecting others' boundaries.

Trust is the belief or confidence that we have in someone or a group of people. This trust is based on our past experiences with them, their reputation, and the information we have collected about them. We can establish trust over time by having positive interactions, being honest and reliable, and maintaining transparency. On the other hand, trust can be broken if someone behaves in a way that goes against our expectations or violates our trust.

In essence, trust is the cornerstone of any successful relationship, whether it's personal or professional. It's crucial for individuals and groups to work together effectively towards a common goal.

Here are six types of trust that are commonly recognized:

- **Contractual Trust:** This is based on formal agreements, contracts, or obligations between parties. It involves trusting someone to fulfill their obligations as stated in the contract or agreement.
- **Competence Trust:** This is based on a person's or group's abilities, skills, and expertise. It involves trusting someone to have the necessary knowledge and skills to perform a task or job.
- **Communication Trust:** This is based on open and honest communication between parties. It involves trusting someone to be transparent and truthful in their communication and to communicate in a timely and appropriate manner.
- **Character Trust:** This type of trust is based on a person's reputation and moral character. It is based on the belief that someone will act with integrity and

honesty, even if there is no oversight or accountability.

- **Care Trust:** Trust that is based on the belief that a person or organization genuinely cares for the well-being of others. This type of trust is often developed through acts of kindness, empathy, and support. Real care means they think about what's best for you, not what's best for them. They have your best interests at heart. They believe in you. They would go above and beyond to support you.
- **Consistency Trust:** One of the most important ways to build trust is to be consistent in your words and actions. This means following through on your commitments, being reliable, and demonstrating that you are dependable.

Be ready to forgive

Forgiveness is an important part of building positive relationships. We all make mistakes, and it's important to be willing to forgive others when they make mistakes too. Forgiveness involves letting go of resentment and anger and choosing to move forward with a positive attitude. When we forgive others, we demonstrate that we value the relationship more than the issue that caused the conflict.

Unforgiveness: Unforgiveness is when a person refuses to forgive someone else, no matter what, even if the person who did wrong apologizes or makes amends. This kind of forgiveness is marked by an absolute unwillingness to forgive and can lead to ongoing feelings of anger, resentment, and bitterness. It's essential to understand that not forgiving can harm mental and emotional health, as well as relationships with others.

Conditional Forgiveness: Conditional forgiveness is a type of forgiveness that is dependent on certain conditions or expectations being met before forgiveness can be granted. This means that there are specific standards that the person who has done wrong must meet before we forgive them. This kind of forgiveness is often associated with a transactional approach, where forgiveness is considered a "deal" between two parties. For instance, "if they say sorry, then I will forgive them." This method may be motivated by the need to prevent future harm and ensure that the person who has done wrong takes responsibility for their actions.

However, conditional forgiveness can also be problematic as it can be used to manipulate or control the situation. This can hinder real healing and reconciliation because the focus is on fulfilling particular conditions rather than working on understanding and personal growth.

Transactional forgiveness can also come from an impulsive place, where forgiveness is given or withheld based on the intensity of our emotions at the moment. For instance, we may forgive someone else to alleviate our guilt for something we did, rather than because we genuinely want to forgive them.

Decisional Forgiveness: Decisional forgiveness is a conscious and intentional choice to release feelings of anger and resentment, or to seek revenge against someone who has harmed you, even if you don’t necessarily feel emotionally ready or willing to forgive them completely. It involves using rational thinking to make a choice to forgive, instead of relying solely on emotions.

With decisional forgiveness, you can decide to forgive someone because it’s the right thing to do, or because holding on to negative emotions is doing more harm than good. This doesn't necessarily mean that you have forgotten the harm that was done, or that you have reconciled with the person who hurt you. Making a decision to forgive can be a helpful step towards emotional forgiveness, which involves truly releasing negative emotions and replacing them with positive ones, such as empathy or compassion.

Emotional Forgiveness: Emotional forgiveness is a process where you work on releasing negative emotions towards someone who has hurt you. This can be hard, as it requires you to reflect on your feelings, show empathy, and try to understand the perspective of the person who caused you pain. It's important to recognize and acknowledge your hurt and pain, and then work on letting go of those negative emotions. This doesn't mean forgetting what happened or accepting bad behavior, but rather finding a way to move forward with positive emotions like compassion and understanding. Emotional forgiveness can have many benefits, like improving your relationships with others, reducing stress, and boosting your self-esteem.

Transformational Forgiveness: Transformational forgiveness goes beyond our typical understanding of forgiveness. It's a process where we transform ourselves by embracing our highest values like love, compassion, and empathy. This kind of forgiveness requires us to let go of negative emotions like anger and resentment towards the person who hurt us. Instead, we approach the situation with an open and curious mind. We try to understand the other person's perspective and see their humanity, acknowledging that they too can make mistakes. We don't depend on an apology or any other action from the offender to forgive them. Instead, we choose to let go of our negative feelings and move towards a more positive and peaceful state of mind. While it may be challenging to practice this kind of forgiveness in severe cases where the offender shows no remorse, it can be liberating as we take control of our emotions and turn our pain into something positive. This kind of forgiveness can help us see the world in a more positive and compassionate way, develop greater empathy, understanding, and connection with others, and ultimately lead to personal growth and fulfillment.

However, here are some general steps that may be helpful:

- **Acknowledge your hurt:** It's important to recognize and acknowledge the pain and hurt caused by the person who has hurt you. Allow yourself to feel the emotions associated with the hurt, but avoid getting stuck in negative emotions such as anger, resentment, or revenge.
- **Shift your perspective:** Instead of seeing the person who hurt you as an enemy or villain, try to see them as a human being who is capable of making mistakes. Recognize that they may have acted out of fear, ignorance, or pain.
- **Cultivate empathy:** Try to put yourself in the shoes of the person who hurt you. Imagine what it would be like to be in their situation and feel their pain. This can help you develop a greater sense of empathy and understanding toward them.
- **Let go of negative emotions:** Forgiveness involves letting go of negative emotions such as anger, resentment, and revenge. This can be challenging, but it is essential to moving towards a more positive and peaceful state of mind.

- **Choose forgiveness:** Forgiveness is a choice, and it is important to choose it deliberately and consciously. Recognize that forgiveness is a gift you give to yourself, not to the person who hurt you.
- **Practice self-compassion:** Forgiveness can be challenging, and it's important to practice self-compassion throughout the process. Be kind and patient with yourself, and recognize that forgiveness is a journey, not a destination.

Unconditional Forgiveness: Unconditional forgiveness is a level of forgiveness in which a person chooses to forgive someone regardless of the severity of the offense or whether the offender has shown any remorse or made any effort to make amends. It is a level of forgiveness that is not based on any conditions or expectations, but rather it comes from a place of love, compassion, and understanding.

Parents often exemplify unconditional forgiveness towards their children because they love them unconditionally. Even if a child makes mistakes, causes harm, or goes against the wishes of their parents, the parent still loves them and forgives them.

Love Languages

Love language is a term that was made popular by Dr. Gary Chapman's book "The 5 Love Languages". It's a way of describing the different ways people show and receive love in romantic relationships. Dr. Chapman identified five main love languages: words of affirmation, acts of service, receiving gifts, quality time, and physical contact.

Every individual has a primary love language, which is how they prefer to receive love from their partner. For example, a person whose primary love language is acts of service may feel more loved when their partner helps them with household or other chores. It's important for couples to understand each other's primary love language and communicate with each other to strengthen their relationship and meet each other's emotional needs.

Words of affirmation: One of the five love languages is words of affirmation, which involves using words to express affection and love. People whose primary love language is words of affirmation feel most loved and appreciated when their partner uses kind, positive, and uplifting words to show their love.

Examples of words of affirmation include expressing gratitude for things your partner does, complimenting them on their character traits or appearance, saying "I love you," or encouraging them in their aspirations. Words of affirmation can be communicated in writing, spoken, or even through text messages or social media. It's important to ensure that your affirmations are specific and genuine and that your partner feels valued and appreciated.

Act of service: Acts of service are one of the five ways people show love to their partners, and it involves doing things for them as a way of expressing love and appreciation. For those whose primary love language is acts of service, they feel most loved and valued when their partner helps them with tasks or chores, takes care of them when they're feeling unwell or stressed, or does something to make their life easier or more enjoyable.

Examples of acts of service include cooking a meal, doing the laundry, running errands, cleaning the house, taking care of the kids or pets, or doing any other task that helps your partner. It's important to make sure that the acts of service you do are significant to your partner and that you're doing them out of a genuine desire to help, rather than out of obligation. Acts of service can be a powerful way to demonstrate your love and appreciation to your partner and to show that you're committed to making their life better.

Receiving gifts: One of the ways people express love and affection is by exchanging gifts, which is known as the receiving gifts love language. Those who prefer this love language feel most loved and appreciated when their partner gives them thoughtful and meaningful gifts that demonstrate they've been thinking of them.

The value of gifts doesn't depend on their cost but rather on the thought and effort behind them. The gifts should be significant and applicable to your partner's interests, needs, and desires. This can range from a simple gift like a favorite book, a bouquet, or a piece of jewelry to something more elaborate, such as a surprise trip or a special experience. However, it's important to note that not everyone considers receiving gifts to be their primary love language, and they may feel loved and appreciated in other ways. It's crucial to understand your partner's love language and communicate your love and appreciation in a way that is significant to them.

Quality time: Spending quality time with your partner is one of the five love languages, where you focus on building an emotional connection by giving them your undivided attention. This can include activities like going for a walk, watching a movie, or enjoying a shared hobby. Quality time is not about spending every moment together, but about intentionally setting aside meaningful time for each other, without distractions or interruptions. It can deepen your emotional bond, build trust, and show your partner how much you value them.

Physical touch: One of the five love languages is physical touch, which involves using physical expressions of affection to show love and appreciation. People whose primary love language is physical touch feel most loved when they receive physical expressions of affection from their partner, such as hugs, kisses, holding hands, or sexual intimacy. Physical touch can vary from small gestures like a hand on the shoulder to more intimate actions like cuddling or sexual intimacy. It's important to understand your partner's primary love language and to communicate your love and appreciation in ways that are meaningful to them. Physical touch should always be consensual and respectful, and it's important to communicate openly and honestly with your partner about your boundaries and preferences. Physical touch can be a powerful way to deepen your emotional connection, build intimacy, and show your partner that you love and care for them.

Building Healthy Relationships

Building healthy relationships involves cultivating positive connections with others on the basis of mutual respect, trust, and support.

Some ways to create healthy relationships as follows:

- Be present and attentive when you spend time with others
- Show empathy and understanding
- Be honest and transparent in communication
- Respecting boundaries and needs

- Celebrate each other's successes and support each other through challenges
- Invest time and effort into maintaining the relationship

Communicate effectively

Effective communication is key to building positive relationships. This involves being clear and direct in our communication while being respectful and attentive to the other person's feelings. We should strive to be good listeners, ask questions when we don't understand something, and avoid making assumptions about what others are thinking or feeling.

Some ways for effective communication are:

- Actively listening to the other person and acknowledging their thoughts and feelings
- Be clear and direct in your communication
- Use "I" statements to express your own thoughts and feelings, rather than blaming or accusing the other person
- Avoiding defensiveness or hostility, even when discussing difficult topics
- Asking questions to clarify understanding and avoid making assumptions
- Be open to feedback and willing to work together to find solutions

CHAPTER EIGHT

FINANCIAL MANAGEMENT

"Money moves from those who do not manage it to those who do." — Dave Ramsey

Money is an essential aspect of our lives, and managing it effectively is crucial for a comfortable and secure future. Financial management is the process of planning, organizing, directing, and controlling the financial activities of an individual or organization. In this chapter, we will explore the fundamentals of financial management and provide some tips to help you take charge of your finances

Warren Buffett is a well-known American investor, business magnate, and philanthropist, who is highly respected for his financial management skills. He is the CEO and largest shareholder of Berkshire Hathaway, a multinational conglomerate holding company. Buffett is an expert in value investing, which involves investing in undervalued companies with strong long-term growth potential. He has also famously said, "Rule No. 1: Never lose money. Rule No. 2: Never forget rule No.1."

One example of Buffett's financial management skills is his investment in American Express in the 1960s when the company was facing financial challenges due to a fraud scandal. Despite the reluctance of other investors, Buffett saw potential for long-term growth and invested in the company, which turned out to be one of Berkshire Hathaway's most successful investments.

Another example of Buffett's financial management skills is his personal frugality. Despite being one of the wealthiest individuals in the world, Buffett is known for living a modest lifestyle and avoiding lavish expenditures. He famously still lives in the same house he purchased in 1958 for $31,500 and is known for his love of fast food and soda. Warren Buffett's financial management skills have earned him the reputation as one of the most successful investors of all time.

Building wealth and saving for the future is a critical aspect of personal finance. It requires careful planning, discipline, and a long-term perspective. Determine what you want to achieve financially and set specific, measurable goals. This could include saving for retirement, buying a home, or paying off debt. Develop a budget that aligns with your financial goals and helps you prioritize your spending. Make sure to allocate funds for savings and investments. Set up automatic savings contributions, so you're paying yourself first before spending on other expenses. This will help ensure that you're consistently saving for the future. Invest your savings in a diversified portfolio of assets that aligns with your risk tolerance and investment objectives. Avoid taking on excessive debt, and pay off high-interest debts as quickly as possible. This will free up more funds for savings and investments. Building wealth and saving for the future requires discipline and consistency. Stick to your budget and savings plan, and resist the temptation to overspend or make impulsive financial decisions.

Set Financial Goals

To manage your finances effectively, the first thing you should do is set financial goals. Here are some tips to help you set financial goals that work:

Figure out what matters to you and what you want to achieve financially. This might include paying off debt, saving for a down payment on a home, or investing for retirement.

Be specific about your goals. Make them measurable, achievable, relevant, and time-bound. Instead of saying "I want to save money," set a goal like "I want to save $5,000 for a down payment on a home within the next year."

Break down your goals into smaller, more manageable steps. For example, if you want to save $100,000 for retirement, set smaller goals of saving $10,000 per year for the next 10 years.

Think about your timeline. If you plan to retire in 30 years, you need to start saving for retirement now. If you want to buy a home in five years, start saving for a down payment now.

Prioritize your goals based on importance and urgency. Start with the most critical goals, like paying off high-interest debt or building an emergency fund, before moving on to less critical goals.

Create a Budget

Creating a budget is a crucial part of managing your money effectively. To get started, calculate your monthly income from your job, any side hustles, or other sources. Next, list all of your monthly expenses, including fixed expenses like rent/mortgage, utilities, car payments, insurance, and groceries, as well as variable expenses like entertainment, dining out, and shopping. Categorize your expenses into essential and non-essential categories, such as housing, food, transportation, healthcare, and optional spending. Allocate your income to cover your expenses, starting with your essential ones, and prioritize your financial goals like paying off debt or saving for a down payment on a home. If your expenses are more than your income, look for ways to reduce expenses or

increase income. Once you've created your budget, track your spending to ensure you're staying on track. Use a budgeting app or spreadsheet to monitor your expenses and progress. Remember, your budget should be a living document that you adjust regularly to reflect changes in your income or expenses. By creating and sticking to a budget, you can manage your money better, decrease your stress, and accomplish your financial objectives. Don't hesitate to change your budget as needed since it's a tool that enables you to make informed financial decisions.

Control Your Spending

Managing your spending is a crucial part of effective financial management. Start by recognizing the things that make you spend money impulsively, like boredom, stress, or social influence. Once you know your triggers, you can work to avoid or cope with them. As previously mentioned, creating a budget is a fundamental tool for controlling your spending. By setting up a budget and assigning your income to cover your expenses, you can prevent overspending and prioritize your financial objectives. Avoid buying things on a whim by taking a moment to think before making a purchase. Ask yourself if the item is really necessary and if it fits your budget. Controlling your spending becomes easier if you use cash instead of credit cards. Set a budget for discretionary spending, withdraw the cash, and use it for purchases. When the cash runs out, you know that you have reached your spending limit. Delaying instant gratification can also help you avoid impulse purchases and manage your spending. Instead of buying something right away, take a day or two to think about whether you truly need it. Look for cheaper alternatives to expensive activities, such as going for a hike or having a movie night at home instead of going out to a restaurant or the movies. By recognizing your spending triggers, establishing a budget, avoiding impulse purchases, using cash, delaying instant gratification, and finding less expensive activities, you can take control of your spending and attain your financial goals. It is important to remember that managing your spending is not about depriving yourself but about making informed decisions about your money.

Save and Invest

Saving and investing are key parts of managing your finances well. Starting early gives your money more time to grow, even if you're only able to save small amounts. To keep yourself motivated and on track, set specific, measurable, achievable, relevant, and time-bound (SMART) goals for your savings. Whether it's for a down payment on a home, a trip, or an emergency fund, having a specific goal can help you stay focused.

Consider setting up automatic transfers from your checking account to your savings or investment accounts. This makes saving money easier and more automatic. It's also a good idea to set aside some of your savings for an emergency fund that can cover at least three to six months of living expenses. Diversifying your investments can help you manage risk and maximize returns. Think about investing in a mix of stocks, bonds, and mutual funds that match your risk tolerance and financial goals. Keep an eye on your investments and make changes if necessary. By saving and investing consistently, you can build your wealth over time and achieve your financial goals. Remember, saving and investing requires discipline, so make it a habit to save and invest regularly.

Review and Adjust Your Financial Plan

It's important to keep track of your financial plan to make sure you're on the right track. Schedule regular check-ins, like once a year or after a big event, to review your progress and adjust your plan as needed. Keep an eye on your investments and make changes if they're not performing well. Check your credit score regularly and work to improve it if necessary. Your budget should also be updated regularly to reflect changes in your income or expenses. Make sure your goals are still relevant and achievable, and don't be afraid to seek professional advice if you're unsure about what changes to make. By staying on top of your financial plan, you can make sure you're still headed in the right direction and adapt to changes along the way.

CHAPTER NINE

SELF-CARE

"Taking care of yourself doesn't mean me first; it means me too." — L.R. KNOST

Taking care of yourself is an important part of being in charge of your life. Self-care means making your physical, emotional, and mental well-being a priority. Self-care is not selfish, but it is essential for living a healthy, joyful, and satisfying life. In this chapter, we will explore why self-care is crucial and offer some practical tips on how to make it a part of your daily routine. Self-care includes any activities that you intentionally do to promote your mental, emotional, and physical health. It involves taking care of your body and mind to achieve a healthy and balanced lifestyle. Ignoring self-care can result in burnout, anxiety, and other health problems.

Michelle Obama, an American lawyer, author, and former First Lady of the United States, is known for her commitment to self-care. She believes that self-care is especially important for women and people of color who may face additional challenges and stress in their lives.

Michelle Obama shares her personal experiences with burnout and exhaustion, which has helped her emphasize the importance of mental and physical health. She is a strong advocate for exercise and makes it a priority to work out every morning, even if it is only for a few minutes. She believes that exercise helps her manage stress and maintain a positive outlook, and encourages others to make exercise a part of their daily routine. Michelle Obama also practices mindfulness and meditation and has spoken about the benefits of these practices for managing stress and improving mental clarity. She often meditates for a few minutes each day to help her stay focused and calm.

Despite her busy schedule, Michelle Obama makes sure to take time for herself and engage in activities that bring her joy. She loves reading, cooking, and spending time with her loved ones, and believes that it is important to prioritize self-care in order to maintain a healthy balance in life.

Michelle Obama is a strong advocate for self-care, and her commitment to prioritizing her own health and well-being has inspired many others to do the same.

Taking care of yourself is really important! When you practice self-care, you're giving yourself a chance to rest and recharge your body and mind. This is key to feeling good and being able to handle everything life throws your way. Plus, self-care can help you manage stress, feel happier, and improve your relationships with others. Even though it might be tough to make time for self-care when you're busy or taking care of others, it's still really important to try. By investing in yourself and making self-care a priority, you're setting yourself up for a healthier, happier, and more fulfilling life overall.

Physical Health

Taking care of your physical health is vital for your overall well-being. Your physical health affects many aspects of your life, such as energy levels, mood, immune system, and the risk of chronic diseases.

To maintain a healthy body, you need to eat a balanced and nutritious diet that includes fruits, vegetables, whole grains, lean protein, and healthy fats. Processed and sugary foods and drinks should be avoided as they can harm your health in the long run. Regular exercise is also essential for improving your cardiovascular health, and mood, and maintaining a healthy weight. Aim for at least 30 minutes of moderate-intensity exercise most days of the week, such as walking, jogging, cycling, or swimming.

Your body needs enough rest to repair and recharge itself. Get seven to eight hours of sleep each night, and establish a consistent sleep routine to help you fall asleep and wake up at the same time each day. Smoking, excessive drinking, and drug use can harm your health and increase the risk of chronic diseases.

Stress can negatively affect your physical health, leading to high blood pressure, heart disease, and other health problems. Develop healthy coping mechanisms such as meditation, yoga, deep breathing, or talking to a therapist to manage stress. Remember that taking care of your physical health is a crucial part of self-care and can lead to a healthier and happier life.

Relaxation

It's important to give yourself a break and relax every day. You can try different things to help you unwind, like meditating, reading, taking a bath, or just sitting quietly and breathing deeply. Relaxation is a vital part of self-care that can help you manage stress, reduce anxiety, and feel more calm and content. By taking the time to relax, you can improve your physical and mental health, and feel more centered and balanced. Mindfulness means paying attention to the present moment without judging yourself. It's a great way to feel more engaged in your daily life, reduce stress and anxiety, and feel more focused. You can practice mindfulness by meditating, doing yoga, or simply taking a few moments each day to concentrate on your breath and the sensations in your body. Taking short breaks throughout the day can also help you recharge and feel less stressed.

You can stretch, go for a walk, or sit quietly and take deep breaths. Doing things you enjoy, like reading, painting, gardening, or spending time in nature, can also help you relax and unwind. Taking a warm bath can be especially soothing after a long day. You might want to try adding some Epsom salt, essential oils, or bath bombs to make the experience even more relaxing.

Engage in activities that bring you joy

It's important to do things that bring you happiness and joy, whether it's spending time outdoors, listening to music, or pursuing a hobby. Engaging in activities that make you happy is a crucial part of taking care of yourself. Not only can it improve your mood, reduce stress, and increase your overall sense of well-being, but it can also help you feel more fulfilled and energized.

To start, think about what activities bring you joy. It could be anything from creative pursuits to sports to music.

Write down a list of the activities you enjoy and consider how you can incorporate them into your daily life. Make sure to set aside time in your schedule for these activities, whether it's dedicating an hour each day to a favorite hobby or planning a fun outing with friends or family. Trying new things is a great way to discover new interests and find new sources of joy, so consider taking a class, learning a new skill, or trying a new hobby.

Focusing on the positive aspects of your life can also help you feel more joyful and content. Take some time each day to reflect on the things you're grateful for and make an effort to appreciate the small moments of joy in your life. Engaging in activities with others can also increase your sense of joy and connection. Consider joining a group focused on a shared interest or spending time with friends and family doing activities that you all enjoy. Remember, prioritizing activities that bring you joy is a vital part of self-care and living a fulfilling life.

Practicing Self-compassion

Be kind to yourself and avoid criticizing or talking negatively about yourself. Practicing self-compassion means treating yourself with care and understanding, just as you would a close friend. This is an important part of taking care of yourself and developing a more compassionate relationship with yourself.

When you notice negative thoughts, challenge them by asking yourself if they're helpful or true. Replace them with more positive and uplifting messages. Remember that everyone makes mistakes, and learn to forgive yourself and move on. Seeking support

from friends, family, or mental health professionals can also help you practice self-compassion.
Make self-compassion a priority in your life, and you'll develop a more positive and accepting relationship with yourself. It's an essential part of self-care and taking charge of your life.

How to handle negative self-talk?

Spot, stop, and swap are simple but effective techniques that can help us to deal with negativity in our life.

- **Spot:** The first step is to spot the negativity when it arises. This means becoming aware of the negative thoughts, emotions, or behaviors that you're experiencing. You can do this by paying attention to your thoughts and feelings throughout the day, and noticing when they turn negative.
- **Stop:** The next step is to stop the negativity in its tracks. This means interrupting the negative thought pattern or behavior as soon as you notice it. One way to do this is to take a deep breath and consciously choose to shift your focus to something positive.
- **Swap:** The final step is to swap negativity for positivity. This means replacing the negative thought or behavior with a more positive one. For example, if you catch yourself thinking negative thoughts about yourself, you can consciously choose to think positive thoughts instead, such as affirmations or statements of gratitude.

Remember, the key to making this technique work is to practice it consistently. The more you spot, stop, and swap, the easier it will become to break the cycle of negativity and cultivate a more positive mindset.

Self-forgiveness

Sometimes, when we look back at things we've done in the past, we might feel ashamed or guilty. This is because we have grown and changed, and the things we did back then don't reflect who we are now. This is actually a good thing because it means we've made progress. We can learn from our past mistakes and become better people. Self-forgiveness means being kind to ourselves and letting go of negative feelings like guilt and shame. It's not always easy, but it can help us grow and heal. To forgive ourselves, we need to accept and take responsibility for our mistakes, and try to make things right if we can. We should also remember that we're not defined by our past mistakes and that everyone makes mistakes. We can learn from our past to create a better future.

Self-forgiveness doesn't mean forgetting what we did or pretending it didn't happen. It means acknowledging our mistakes, learning from them, and using that knowledge to become a better person.

Gratitude

Gratitude is all about being thankful and appreciative of the good things and people in our lives. It's about recognizing and cherishing the positive things, big or small, such as a beautiful sunset, a good book, or a warm cup of coffee.

The practice of gratitude has many benefits for our physical and mental health, such as lower stress and depression levels, improved relationships, and better sleep. It helps us develop a positive outlook and appreciate the good in our lives, even during tough times. Gratitude and kindness are closely related. When someone is kind to us, it can inspire feelings of gratitude toward that person. Likewise, when we are kind to others, it can cultivate feelings of gratitude within ourselves.

Showing kindness towards others is a way of expressing our appreciation and gratitude for them. This creates a positive cycle, where acts of kindness and expressions of gratitude reinforce each other. For instance, when someone does something kind for us, we may express our gratitude and appreciation, which can make them feel good and encourage them to continue to be kind to others.

Expressing gratitude can take different forms and be directed toward various aspects of our lives. **Gratitude can be expressed in two ways: Generic and Specific.**

Generic gratitude is a general sense of appreciation for the good things in life, such as good health, supportive relationships, and the beauty of nature. It is not tied to a specific event or person.

Specific gratitude, on the other hand, is more focused and personalized, directed towards a specific event, person, or action that has positively impacted our lives. It can be directed towards a friend who provided support during a difficult time, a mentor who offered guidance and encouragement, or a family member who supported our aspirations.

Gratitude can also be categorized into three common types: Gratitude for the self, gratitude for life, and gratitude for the world. Gratitude for the self involves acknowledging our own strengths and accomplishments. Gratitude for life involves appreciating the positive experiences, relationships, and opportunities that we encounter in life. Gratitude for the world involves recognizing the interconnectedness of all things and feeling grateful for the positive contributions and actions of others.

Experiencing gratitude involves several stages of processing and emotions that are common.

Here are the different stages of gratitude:

- **Recognize the Good:** The first stage of gratitude is simply noticing the good things in our lives. This could be as simple as acknowledging a beautiful sunset, feeling grateful for a kind gesture from a friend, or appreciating a comfortable bed to sleep in. This initial stage helps us shift our attention away from negative thoughts and towards the positive aspects of our lives.
- **Acknowledge the Good:** After recognizing the good things in our lives, the next stage is to acknowledge and appreciate them. This means taking time to reflect on what we're grateful for and expressing our gratitude. We might write in a gratitude journal, thank someone who has helped us, or take a moment to savor a positive experience.
- **Deepen Appreciation the Good:** In the third stage of gratitude, we deepen our appreciation for the good things in our lives. This involves recognizing the value and significance of positive experiences and cultivating a sense of awe and wonder. For instance, we might admire the beauty of a natural landscape or feel incredibly grateful for the love and support of our friends and family.
- **Express Gratitude:** The final stage of gratitude is expressing our appreciation and thankfulness to others. This can be done through simple acts of kindness, such as offering a heartfelt "thank you" to someone who has helped us, or more formal expressions of gratitude, such

as writing a letter or making a donation in someone's honor. By expressing our gratitude, we not only deepen our own sense of appreciation but also foster positive connections and relationships with others.

Meditation

Meditation is a technique that involves concentration on a specific object, idea or task in order to achieve a state of mental clarity and tranquility. It has been practiced for thousands of years in different cultures and spiritual practices with the aim of achieving greater awareness, inner peace, and relaxation.

Typically, during meditation, individuals sit or lie down in a quiet environment and concentrate on their breath, a particular sound or a visual image. Through this practice, they may experience a reduction in distracting thoughts and feelings of stress or anxiety.

Meditation has been linked to a range of mental and physical benefits, including decreased stress, improved concentration, better emotional control, and lower blood pressure. There are many types of meditation, each with their own specific focus and techniques, and it is accessible to individuals of all ages and backgrounds.

Mindfulness Meditation: This type of meditation involves focusing your attention on your breath or bodily sensations while observing your thoughts and emotions without judgment.

Here are the basic steps:

- Sit in a comfortable position with your back straight, and close your eyes or keep them slightly open.

- Focus your attention on your breath, feeling the sensations of each inhale and exhale.
- If your mind wanders, simply observe the thought without judgment and bring your attention back to your breath.
- Continue this practice for a set amount of time, such as 10 or 20 minutes.

Diaphragmatic Breathing: Also known as belly breathing, this technique involves breathing deeply into the diaphragm, which is the muscle that separates the chest from the abdomen.

Here are the basic steps:

- Sit or lie down in a comfortable position.
- Place one hand on your chest and the other on your belly.
- Inhale deeply through your nose, feeling your belly rise and expand.
- Exhale slowly through your mouth, feeling your belly fall and contract.
- Repeat for several minutes.

Box Breathing

Here are the basic steps:

- Sit or stand in a comfortable position.
- Inhale deeply through your nose for a count of four.
- Hold your breath for a count of four.
- Exhale slowly through your mouth for a count of four.
- Hold your breath for a count of four.
- Repeat for several minutes.

CHAPTER TEN

THINKING

"The thinking that got us to where we are is not the thinking that will get us where we want to be." — Albert Einstein

As human beings, we possess the ability to think, reason, and make decisions. Our brains, specifically the neocortex, are responsible for these cognitive processes. The neocortex is the outer layer of the brain and is involved in higher-order thinking, including language, perception, and consciousness. In this chapter, we will explore how the neocortex influences our thinking and how we can use mental models to improve our decision-making abilities.

Charlie Munger is widely regarded as one of the greatest thinkers and investors of our time. He is best known as the vice chairman of Berkshire Hathaway, the multinational conglomerate holding company led by Warren Buffett. Munger is known for his exceptional intellect, his wisdom, and his unique approach to decision-making.

He was born in Omaha, Nebraska in 1924 and went on to study mathematics at the University of Michigan. After serving in the U.S. Army Air Corps during World War II,

Munger attended Harvard Law School and later worked as a lawyer and investor. Munger's strength as a thinker lies in his ability to combine knowledge from various fields, such as psychology, economics, biology, and physics, to better understand the world. He believes that by building a network of interconnected mental models, one can gain a better perspective and make better decisions.

Munger also emphasizes the importance of rational thinking and avoiding common biases that can affect our judgment. He encourages "inversion," which involves thinking about a problem in reverse order to gain insight into what actions are necessary to achieve a desired outcome.

Munger's thinking has had a significant impact on Berkshire Hathaway, where he serves as the vice chairman, and the investing world. He is highly respected for his emphasis on long-term thinking and multidisciplinary thinking. Investors around the world eagerly anticipate his annual appearances at Berkshire Hathaway's shareholder meetings.

Charlie Munger's story as a thinker is one of curiosity, disciplined thinking, and a commitment to lifelong learning. His approach to decision-making and his unique insights into the world have made him a highly influential figure in business and investing.

The Neocortex

The neocortex is a part of the brain that is divided into different regions, each with specific functions. The prefrontal cortex, which is located in the front part of the brain, is responsible for decision-making, problem-solving, and planning. The parietal cortex, located towards the top and back of the brain, helps us to be aware of our surroundings and perceive what we see, hear, and feel. The temporal cortex, located towards the sides of the brain, is important for language and memory. Lastly, the occipital cortex, located at the back of the brain, processes what we see.

All of these regions work together to help us think and perceive the world around us. Whenever we face a problem or situation, the neocortex takes in information, compares it to our past experiences, and creates possible solutions. Additionally, the neocortex also uses feedback from our senses to make judgments and decisions.

Mental Models

Our neocortex is incredibly powerful, but it can also be prone to biases and errors. Mental models can help us overcome these limitations by providing a framework for thinking and decision-making. A mental model is a cognitive framework or representation that a person uses to organize, understand, and make sense of the world around them. Mental models can be thought of as internal, conceptual models that people use to interpret and interact with the environment.

First principles thinking

First principles thinking is a problem-solving method where we break down big problems into small, simple parts and then put them back together from the bottom up. It's a way of thinking that encourages us to question our assumptions and find new and better ways of solving problems.

A great example of first principles thinking is Elon Musk, who used it to make reusable rockets for SpaceX. Instead of accepting that rockets had to be expensive to make, he broke down the problem and asked why each component was so costly. Then he found ways to make the parts cheaper or create a new and better way of making them. By doing this, he made space travel more affordable.

To use first principles thinking, we need to follow these steps: First, we identify the problem we want to solve. Then we break it down into its most basic parts. After that, we challenge our assumptions about the problem and create new solutions based on the fundamental parts. Finally, we test and improve our solution based on feedback.

In conclusion, first-principle thinking helps us solve complex problems by breaking them down into simple parts and finding new and innovative solutions. By understanding the basic principles of a problem, we can challenge assumptions and come up with better ways of achieving our goals.

5 Whys

The Five Whys is a mental model used to identify the root cause of a problem by asking "why" repeatedly until the root cause is identified. It is a simple but powerful method for identifying the underlying cause of a problem and finding effective solutions. This technique is used in many different fields, including manufacturing, engineering, and problem-solving.

Here's an example of how the Five Whys can be used to identify the root cause of a problem:

Problem: The company's sales have been declining for the past few months.

- Why are sales declining? - Because our marketing campaigns aren't generating as much interest as they used to.
- Why aren't the marketing campaigns generating as much interest? - Because our target audience is changing and our campaigns aren't keeping up.
- Why aren't our campaigns keeping up with our target audience? - Because we haven't done enough research to understand their changing preferences and behaviors.
- Why haven't we done enough research? - Because we've been relying on outdated market research and haven't invested in new research methods.
- Why haven't we invested in new research methods? - Because we don't have the budget for it.

In this example, the root cause of the declining sales is the lack of budget to invest in new research methods to understand the changing preferences and behaviors of the target audience. By asking "why" five times, we were able to identify the root cause of the problem and come up with a potential solution.

The Five Whys is an effective tool because it encourages teams to focus on solving the underlying cause of a problem. It can be applied to different types of issues, from simple to complex challenges, and can be used for personal and professional problem-solving. By using this method, s and teams can identify the root cause of a problem and work toward a long-term solution.

Second-Order Thinking

Second-order thinking, also known as second-level thinking or second-level reasoning, is a mental model that involves thinking beyond the immediate or obvious consequences of a decision or action and considering the longer-term or indirect effects. This approach can help you anticipate unintended consequences and make better decisions. In other words, it involves thinking beyond the surface-level impacts of a choice to understand the potential ripple effects.

Here's an example of how second-order thinking can be used to make a better decision:

Problem: You're considering investing in a high-growth tech startup.

- **First-order thinking:** The startup has a lot of potential for growth and could provide a high return on investment.
- **Second-order thinking:** Investing in the startup could also mean exposing yourself to a high level of risk, especially if the company is unable to sustain its growth or faces unexpected challenges. It could also mean tying up your capital in a long-term investment that may be difficult to sell or exit.

By using second-order thinking, you are considering not just the immediate benefits of an investment opportunity, but also the potential risks and longer-term consequences. In this example, you might decide that the potential risks outweigh the potential benefits of the investment, and choose to invest in a less risky but also less potentially rewarding opportunity.

Another example of second-order thinking is environmental conservation. By considering the long-term effects of actions on the environment, people s and organizations can make better decisions about how to use natural resources and how to reduce their environmental impact. While actions like cutting down trees or using fossil fuels might provide short-term benefits, their long-term effects on the environment could have serious consequences for future generations.

Second-order thinking involves considering the long-term and indirect consequences of a decision or action, beyond the immediate benefits or risks. By using this mental model, people s and organizations can make more informed decisions and anticipate unintended consequences, improving their ability to achieve their goals and avoid potential problems.

Inversion Thinking

Inversion thinking is a mental model that involves thinking about a problem or challenge in reverse, by considering what you don't want to happen, rather than what you do want to happen. This approach can help you identify potential obstacles or pitfalls and find ways to avoid them.

Here's an example of how inversion thinking can be used to solve a problem:

Problem: You want to start a new business, but you're not sure how to ensure its success. Instead of asking, "What can I do to make my business successful?", ask, "What could cause my business to fail?"

Potential answers to this question might include things like a lack of market demand, an inability to compete with established businesses, or a shortage of skilled employees. Once you've identified potential causes of failure, you can work on strategies to mitigate these risks and improve your chances of success.

In this example, inversion thinking helped the entrepreneur to identify potential obstacles to the success of their business and come up with strategies to address them. By considering what they don't want to happen, rather than just what they do want to happen, they were able to approach the problem from a different perspective and gain new insights.

Inversion thinking can be applied to many different types of problems and challenges, and it can help to reveal hidden assumptions or biases that might be limiting your thinking. By considering what you don't want to happen, you can identify potential risks and develop strategies to mitigate them, improving your chances of success.

Pareto Principle

The Pareto Principle, also known as the 80/20 rule, is a concept used in economics and business management that states that roughly 80% of the effects come from 20% of the causes.

The idea was originally proposed by an Italian economist named Vilfredo Pareto, who observed that 80% of the land in Italy was owned by just 20% of the population.

In business, the Pareto Principle can be applied to many areas, such as sales, customer service, and productivity. For example, a company might find that 80% of its sales come from just 20% of its customers, or that 80% of its customer complaints come from just 20% of its products.

By identifying and focusing on the 20% of causes that generate 80% of the effects, companies can allocate their resources more efficiently and effectively. This allows them to achieve more with less, and to prioritize their efforts in the areas that will have the biggest impact.

For instance, consider a retail store that sells a range of products. The store managers may notice that 80% of their sales come from just 20% of their products. By focusing on these products and optimizing their display and promotion, the store can increase its sales and profits while reducing waste and inefficiency in its operations. In another example, a software company may find that 80% of their customer complaints come from just 20% of their features. By identifying and improving these features, they can improve customer satisfaction and reduce support costs, which can lead to greater long-term success.

The Pareto Principle suggests that a small percentage of causes can generate a large percentage of effects and that by focusing on these key areas, companies can achieve greater efficiency, effectiveness, and success.

Circle Of Competence

The "circle of competence" is a mental model that was developed by investor Warren Buffett to help people s make better decisions about where to invest their time and resources. The Circle of Competence is a mental model that suggests that people s should focus their efforts on areas where they have knowledge, skills, and expertise, and avoid areas where they lack these competencies. It's a way of defining the boundaries of what we know and don't know so that we can make better decisions and allocate our resources more effectively. This can help people s make more informed decisions, avoid costly mistakes, and ultimately achieve greater success.

For example, suppose you're an investor who specializes in the technology industry. Your circle of competence would include companies that operate in this sector, such as software firms, hardware manufacturers, and internet companies. You would have in-depth knowledge of the trends, technologies, and competitive landscape within this industry, which would allow you to make informed investment decisions.

On the other hand, if you lack knowledge in the healthcare industry, it would be outside of your circle of competence. Investing in pharmaceutical or biotech companies without adequate knowledge of the industry's complexities and regulations could result in poor investment decisions.

The circle of competence applies to any area of life where knowledge and expertise are required, from career choices to personal hobbies. By recognizing our strengths and limitations and focusing on areas where we have a competitive advantage, we can make

better decisions and achieve greater success. It's important to periodically reassess our circle of competence and expand it through learning and experience.

Compounding

The compounding mental model refers to the idea that small changes or investments made over a long period of time can have a significant impact due to the power of compounding. This model is particularly relevant to financial investments, but can also be applied to a wide range of other areas.

Here is an example of the compounding mental model:
Example: Investment
Suppose you have $10,000 to invest. You decide to invest this money in a stock market index fund that returns an average of 7% per year. If you were to leave this money

untouched for 30 years, it would grow to approximately $76,122 assuming the 7% annual return is maintained.

However, if you were to add just $100 to this investment every month, the impact of compounding would be significant. Over 30 years, this additional investment of $100 per month would result in a total investment of $46,000 but would grow to approximately $193,067 assuming the 7% annual return is maintained.

This is an example of the power of compounding. By making small, consistent investments over a long period of time, the impact of each investment is magnified by the compounding effect, resulting in a much larger overall return.

The compounding mental model is useful not only for financial investments but also for personal development and goal setting. By making small, consistent efforts over a long period of time, people s can achieve significant progress and growth. For example, a person who wants to learn a new language could commit to studying for just 30 minutes each day, and over time the cumulative effect of this small daily effort would result in significant progress.

Entropy

Entropy is a measure of the amount of disorder or randomness in a system. It is a concept that is commonly used in thermodynamics to describe the behavior of physical systems, but it can also be applied to other systems in which there is a degree of disorder or randomness.

Here is an example of the entropy mental model:

Example: A room

Consider a room that is initially clean and organized. Over time, if no one cleans or organizes the room, it will become more and more disordered, with items scattered about and dust accumulating on surfaces. This increase in disorder is an example of entropy in action.

From a thermodynamic perspective, the energy in the room is becoming more evenly distributed as it is converted from potential energy (such as the organization of items in the room) to kinetic energy (such as the movement of dust particles). This increase in disorder and decrease in potential energy is reflected in the increase in entropy of the system.

In this example, we can see that entropy is a measure of the degree of disorder or randomness in a system. As the room becomes more disordered, the entropy of the system increases. Similarly, in thermodynamic systems, entropy increases as energy is converted from one form to another, leading to an increase in the degree of disorder or randomness in the system.

Decision-making: The 40/70 Rule

The 40/70 mental model is a decision-making framework that suggests that you should make a decision when you have between 40% and 70% of the information you need. Waiting for more information beyond 70% can lead to analysis paralysis and missed opportunities while making decisions with less than 40% of the information can lead to poor choices.

An example of the 40/70 mental model in action might be a business executive who is considering a new investment opportunity. They have done some initial research and analysis, but they don't yet have all of the information they need to make a final decision. According to the 40/70 rule, they should make a decision based on the information they have at hand, as long as it falls within the 40-70% range. If they wait until they have more than 70% of the information, they might miss out on the opportunity, as others may have already acted on it. On the other hand, if they make a decision with less than 40% of the information, they may be taking too big of a risk without fully understanding the potential downsides.

Key takeways from the 40/70 rule include:

- **Don't wait for perfect information:** In many cases, it's not possible or practical to wait until you have all the information you need to make a decision. The 40/70 rule encourages you to make a decision based on the information you have, rather than waiting for perfect information that may never arrive.
- **Avoid analysis paralysis:** Waiting for more information beyond the 70% mark can lead to analysis paralysis, where you become stuck in the decision-making process and fail to take action. By focusing on the information you have, you can avoid this pitfall. Manage risk: Making decisions with less than 40% of the information can be risky, as you may not fully understand the potential downsides. By using the 40/70 rule, you can manage risk and avoid taking unnecessary risks.
- **Continuously reassess your decision:** The 40/70 rule is not a one-time decision-making process. Instead, it's an ongoing process of reassessing your decision as new information becomes available. By doing this, you can adjust your decision as needed and minimize the risk of making a poor choice.

The 40/70 mental model is a useful framework for making decisions when you don't have all the information you need. By focusing on the information you have, managing risk, and continuously reassessing your decision, you can make informed choices and avoid analysis paralysis.

By using mental models, we can think more clearly and make better decisions. Mental models can help us identify patterns, recognize biases, and consider different perspectives. They can also help us avoid common cognitive traps, such as confirmation bias and sunk cost fallacy.

To apply mental models to your life, start by identifying the mental models that are relevant to your goals and interests. For example, if you want to improve your financial literacy, you might focus on mental models related to personal finance, such as compound interest and opportunity cost.

Next, practice using these mental models in your daily life. Look for opportunities to apply them to real-world situations, such as evaluating a job offer or making a big purchase. Over time, using mental models will become more intuitive, and you will start to apply them automatically.

Finally, continue to expand your mental model toolkit by learning about new mental models and applying them to different situations. By continually improving your thinking skills, you can take charge of your life and achieve your goals.

CHAPTER ELEVEN

OVERCOMING OBSTACLES

"The impediment to action advances action. What stands in the way becomes the way." — Marcus Aurelius

Obstacles are an inevitable part of life. Obstacles are challenges that we encounter in life that can prevent us from reaching our goals or desired outcomes. They can come in many forms, such as physical, mental, emotional, and social barriers. However, it is how we respond to these obstacles that can ultimately determine our success in life. In this chapter, we will explore strategies for overcoming obstacles so that you can take charge of your life.

Nick Vujicic is a remarkable man who has been an inspiration to millions of people around the world. He was born without arms and legs, a condition known as tetra-amelia syndrome, which many people would consider an insurmountable obstacle. However, Nick has not only overcome this challenge but has used it to become a powerful motivational speaker, author, and entrepreneur.

Growing up, Nick faced many challenges that most people

take for granted, such as tying their shoes, brushing their teeth, or even getting dressed. He struggled with feelings of loneliness and depression and often felt like an outcast. However, Nick's parents always encouraged him to find ways to overcome his challenges and to believe in himself. Despite his physical limitations, Nick was determined to live a full and meaningful life. He learned to swim, surf, and even play golf. He also found his passion for motivational speaking and began sharing his story with others, inspiring them to overcome their own obstacles and achieve their goals.

Nick's message is simple but powerful: no matter what challenges we face, we can choose to believe in ourselves, stay positive, and never give up. His life story is a testament to the human spirit and the power of resilience.

Through his motivational speeches, books, and businesses, Nick has touched the lives of countless people around the world. He has become a symbol of hope and inspiration for those facing challenges, reminding them that they are capable of achieving their dreams and making a difference in the world.

Nick's story teaches us that the obstacles we face in life do not define us. It is our response to these challenges that define who we are and what we can achieve. By staying positive, believing in ourselves, and never giving up, we too can overcome any obstacle and achieve our goals.

Another example of an obstacle is that of Oprah Winfrey, who faced many challenges on her journey to becoming a media mogul. Oprah Winfrey is one of the most inspiring and influential women in the world, and her life story is nothing short of awe-inspiring. She was born into poverty in rural Mississippi in 1954 and faced numerous obstacles throughout her childhood. Her mother was a teenager when she gave birth to Oprah, and her father was absent from her life. Oprah was raised by her grandmother until she was six years old, and then she moved to Milwaukee to live with her mother.

Despite her difficult upbringing, Oprah showed an early talent for public speaking, winning a number of awards and honors in school. At the age of 14, she landed her first job in radio, working as a news reader for a local radio station. She continued to work in radio and television throughout her teenage years and early 20s, eventually moving to Baltimore to co-anchor the evening news.

It was in 1983, when Oprah moved to Chicago to host a morning talk show called "AM Chicago," that her career really took off. The show was an instant hit, and within a year it had been renamed "The Oprah Winfrey Show" and was broadcast nationally. Over the next 25 years, Oprah became one of the most successful talk show hosts in history, winning numerous awards and accolades for her work.

But Oprah's success was not without its challenges. She faced criticism and controversy throughout her career, including accusations of sensationalism and exploitation. However, Oprah never let her critics get in the way of her vision. She continued to use her platform to address important social and political issues, including racism, poverty, and inequality.

Beyond her talk show, Oprah has also been a successful entrepreneur, launching her own television network, OWN, in 2011. She has also been a philanthropist, donating millions of dollars to charity and starting her own foundation to help empower women and children.

Today, Oprah is one of the most respected and admired women in the world, with a net worth of over $2.6 billion.

Her life story is a testament to the power of resilience, hard work, and determination in the face of adversity.

Both Nick Vujicic and Oprah Winfrey faced significant obstacles in their lives, but they refused to let those obstacles hold them back. Instead, they used their challenges as opportunities to grow and learn, inspiring others along the way. Their stories demonstrate the power of resilience and determination in overcoming obstacles and achieving success.

Why it's important to overcome obstacles

Overcoming obstacles is really important because it helps us grow as people and become more successful. Obstacles are like challenges we face on our path to achieving our goals, and if we don't learn how to overcome them, they can hold us back. When we overcome obstacles, we learn how to be strong and keep going even when things are tough. It also helps us become better problem solvers and more confident in ourselves. Ultimately, overcoming obstacles helps us achieve our goals and be happier in life.

Overcame obstacles

The first step in overcoming any obstacle is to acknowledge its existence. It's easy to ignore or deny the obstacle, hoping it will go away on its own. However, this approach can make the situation worse and can be a significant barrier to finding a solution.

To acknowledge the obstacle, take time to reflect on the situation and identify the problem. Be honest with yourself about the impact the obstacle is having on your life and your goals. This step may be difficult, but it's an essential part of the process. By acknowledging the obstacle, you can begin to take steps to overcome it.

This involves identifying the obstacle, understanding its impact on your life or goals, and accepting that it exists.

To acknowledge the obstacle, you can start by asking yourself:

- What is the obstacle that I am facing?
- How is it affecting me and my goals?
- Am I willing to accept that this obstacle exists?

By answering these questions, we can gain clarity and understanding of the obstacle we are facing, and start to create a plan to overcome it. Remember that acknowledging the obstacle is not about dwelling on it or giving up, but rather about recognizing its presence and taking action to move forward.

Once we've acknowledged the obstacle, the next step is an alternative perspective. An alternative perspective means shifting our perspective to see the obstacle as an opportunity rather than a problem. This can help us stay motivated, positive, and focused on our goals.

Let's say you're an entrepreneur who's just experienced a business failure. It's easy to feel defeated and give up, but alternating your perspective can help you see the obstacle as an opportunity for growth and learning. You can ask yourself questions like "What did I learn from this experience?" or "What can I do differently next time?" to shift your perspective.

For example, you may decide to focus on the skills and knowledge you gained from the failure or use it as motivation to start a new venture with a stronger foundation. An alternative perspective can help us stay motivated, positive, and focused on our goals. Creating a plan of action is the next thing we can do to overcome obstacles. This involves defining your goal, identifying potential solutions, evaluating your options, and creating a plan of action.

To create a plan of action, we must define our goal, brainstorm potential solutions, evaluate the options that we have, and create a step-by-step plan. Remember to stay flexible and open to making changes as you move forward. This step may require research, consultation with others, and trial and error, but it's an essential part of the process.

Taking action is the fourth step in overcoming obstacles. This involves putting our plan of action into motion, staying focused on our goal, staying flexible and adaptable, and adjusting our plan as needed.

For example, if you're a writer struggling to finish a book, the first step is to write a page or even a paragraph. Breaking down the goal into manageable steps can help you stay focused and motivated.

As you take action, stay flexible and adaptable, adjusting your plan as needed. You may encounter obstacles along the way, but the key is to keep moving forward and not give up.

Seeking support is the fifth step in overcoming obstacles. This involves reaching out to others for help, building a support system, surrounding yourself with positivity, and seeking guidance and advice.

To seek support, reach out to others for help, build a support system, surround yourself with positivity, and seek guidance and advice from mentors or professionals. This step may require vulnerability, trust, and a willingness to accept help from others.

Finally, it's crucial to learn from the experience. Reflect on the process, identify lessons learned, and use those lessons to improve yourself and your future actions. For example, if you're an athlete who failed to achieve a personal best time in a race, you can reflect on what went wrong and what you can do differently in your training.

Learning from the experience can help you develop a growth mindset and improve your resilience. Remember that setbacks and failures are opportunities for learning and growth, not signs of weakness or defeat.

To learn from the experience, reflect on the process, identify lessons learned, and use those lessons to improve yourself and your future actions. This step may require self-awareness, introspection, and a willingness to make changes based on what you've learned.

Printed by Libri Plureos GmbH in Hamburg,
Germany